Northfield Public Library
Northfield, Minnesota

Gift Presented by

*Leslie J. Gustafson
Memorial Fund*

I Can Make
MUSICAL INSTRUMENTS

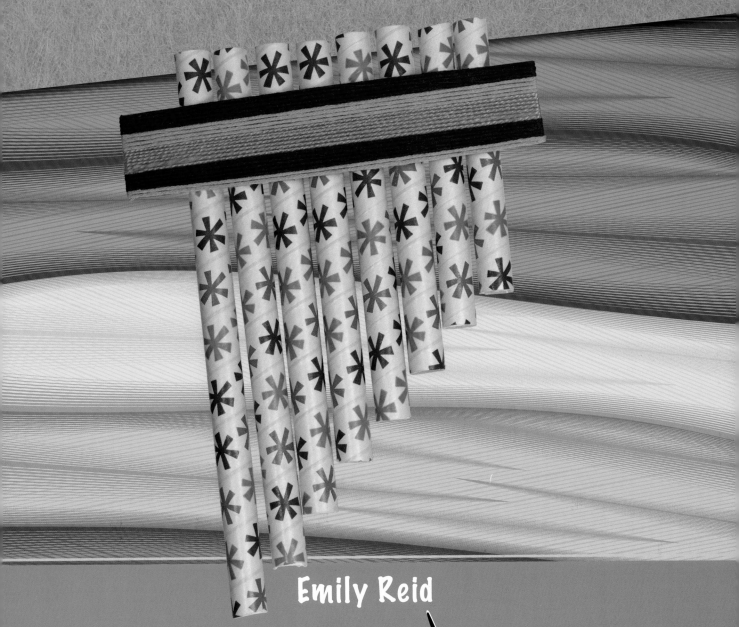

Emily Reid

WINDMILL BOOKS
New York

Published in 2016 by **Windmill Books**, an Imprint of Rosen Publishing
29 East 21st Street, New York, NY 10010

Developed and produced for Rosen by BlueAppleWorks Inc.

Creative Director: Melissa McClellan
Managing Editor for BlueAppleWorks: Melissa McClellan
Designer: T.J. Choleva
Photo Research: Jane Reid
Editor: Janice Dyer
Craft Artisans: Jane Yates (p. 8, 10, 12, 18, 22, 24, 28); Jerrie McClellan (p. 14, 16, 20, 26)

Photo Credits: cover background image, title page background PILart/Shutterstock; cover center image,
cover insets, title page, TOC, p. 6, 8–9, 10–11, 12–13, 14–15, 16–17, 18–19, 20–21, 22–23, 24–25, 26–27, 28-29
Austen Photography; p. 4 left, 5 first row Photka/Dreamstime; p. 4 right top Ermolaevamariya/Dreamstime;
p. 4 right bottom Richard Thomas/Dreamstime; p. 5 first row right Ghassan Safi/Dreamstime; p. 5 first row
bottom Sabrina Cercelovic/Dreamstime; p. 5 second row left tescha555/Thinkstock; p. 5 second row
middle Christian Bertrand/Dreamstime; p. 5 second row right Fuse/Thinkstock; p. 5 third row left Vasily
Kovalev/Dreamstime; p. 5 third row middle Empire331/Dreamstime; p. 5 third row right (left to right)
Crackerclips/Dreamstime; Les Cunliffe/Dreamstime; Jerryb8/Dreamstime; p. 5 fourth row left (left to right)
Merydolla/Dreamstime; azgek/Thinkstock; Stephanie Connell/Dreamstime; p. 5 fourth row right (left to
right clockwise) antpkr/Thinkstock; Peanutroaster/Dreamstime; Onur Ersin/Dreamstime;Jirk4/Dreamstime;
Gradts/Dreamstime; p. 7 top Robyn Mackenzie/Dreamstime; p. 7 bottom left Kesaree Prakumthong/
Dreamstime; p. 9 top right Carlos Caetano/Shutterstock; p. 11 top right Lunamarina/Dreamstime; p. 11
bottom Juan Moyano/Dreamstime; p. 13 top right Gvictoria/Dreamstime; p. 15 top right Radu Razvan
Gheorghe/Dreamstime; p. 17 top right Andres Rodriguez/Dreamstime; p. 19 top right Andrey Gontarev/
Shutterstock; p. 21 top right Konstantin Karchevskiy/Dreamstime; p. 23 top right Cottonfioc/Thinkstock; p. 23
bottom Jacek Chabraszewski/Dreamstime; p. 25 top right HomeStudio/Shutterstock; p. 27 top right Rafał
Cichawa/Dreamstime; p. 27 bottom Dario Lo Presti/Thinkstock; p. 29 top right Peanutroaster/Dreamstime.

Cataloging-in-Publication-Data

Reid, Emily.
I can make musical instruments / by Emily Reid.
p. cm. — (Makerspace projects)
Includes index.
ISBN 978-1-4777-5643-0 (pbk.)
ISBN 978-1-4777-5642-3 (6 pack)
ISBN 978-1-4777-5566-2 (library binding)
1. Musical instruments — Construction — Juvenile literature.
2. Musical instruments — Juvenile literature.
3. Handicraft — Juvenile literature. I. Title.
ML460.R45 2016
784.192'3—d23

Manufactured in the United States of America
CPSIA Compliance Information: Batch #WS15WM: For Further Information contact: Rosen Publishing, New York, New York at 1-800-237-9932

CONTENTS

MATERIALS

A makerspace is a space to think and be creative. You can dedicate a space for your makerspace, or make one as you need it. You may already have many of the basic supplies for your makerspace.

You can purchase whatever else you need at a craft store or dollar store. If you don't have a dedicated area, make a portable makerspace by organizing your supplies in boxes or plastic bins and pull them out when you want to create.

A note about patterns

Many of the musical instruments in this book use patterns or **templates**. Trace the pattern, cut the pattern, and then place it on the material you want to cut out. You can either tape it in place and cut both the pattern and material, or trace around the pattern onto the material and then cut it out.

RECYCLABLES

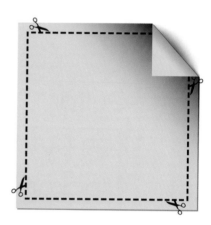

You can make many of the musical instruments in this book with materials found around the house. Save recyclables (newspapers, cardboard boxes, mailing tubes, cereal boxes, tin cans, and more) to use in your craft projects. Use your imagination and have fun!

PAINT, MARKERS, AND PASTELS

CRAFT THREAD

DECORATIVE TAPE

BUTTONS

AIR-DRYING CLAY

RUBBER BANDS

GLUE AND TAPE

PAPER

DOWELS

TOOLS
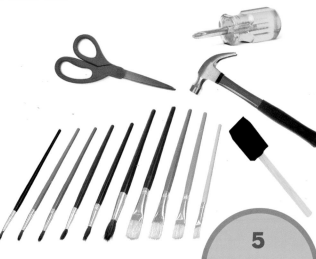

TECHNIQUES

Have fun while making your musical instruments! Be creative. Your project does not have to look just like the one in this book. If you don't have a certain material, think of something similar you could use.

The following techniques will help you create your musical instruments.

MAKING HOLES IN CARDBOARD

Some projects require holes to be made in cardboard. There are several methods.

- Use the tip of a pair of sharp scissors to create the hole. Push the tip of the scissors through the hole and then turn the scissors. If you use this method, always point the scissors away from yourself!

- Small holes — push a nail through the cardboard. Always point the nail away from yourself!

- Medium holes — start with the nail to make a small hole, then push a Phillips screwdriver through the small hole to make it larger.

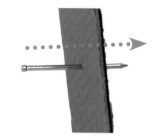

- Big holes — start with the nail to make a small hole, then push a Phillips screwdriver through the small hole to make it larger. Then insert your scissors and cut the hole to the size you want.

BE SAFE

- Ask for help when you need it.
- Ask for permission to borrow tools from others.
- Be careful when using knives, scissors, and sewing needles.

BE PREPARED

- Read through the instructions and make sure you have all the materials you need.
- Cover your work area with newspaper or cardboard.
- Clean up your makerspace when you are finished making your project.

PAINTING

Apply paint to your instrument using a paintbrush or foam brush. Make sure to put newspapers or a flattened cardboard box under your work area.

MAKING PAPER DOWELS

Several crafts in this book use wooden **dowels**. If you don't have one, you can make one with paper. Roll newspaper as tight as you can and then tape to secure it.

USING COLLAGE

You can decorate your instrument using the collage technique. Arrange and glue cut-up pieces of tissue paper, magazine pages or wrapping paper in an interesting pattern. You can also buy specialty glues which can be found in most crafting stores.

- Standard craft glue works best if it is diluted with a little water.

- Use a paintbrush to spread some of the glue onto a small part of your project. Press the paper into the glue.

- When you are finished gluing the paper, cover it with a thin layer of glue to seal the paper.

- Make sure to use glue that dries clear.

FOLDING CARDBOARD

Cardboard is easier to fold if you **score** the fold lines first: Place a ruler along the line you want to fold. Set a blunt tip* on the surface of the cardboard against the ruler. Press and pull the blunt tip along the ruler. Do not cut through the cardboard. Bend the cardboard at the indentation the blunt tip created.

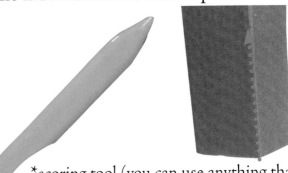

*scoring tool (you can use anything that has a blunt tip: a **retracted** ball point pen, dull pencil, screwdriver)

A note about measurements

Measurements are given in U.S. form with metric in brackets. The metric conversion is rounded to make it easier to measure.

Creating a craft from materials using your creativity is a very rewarding activity. When you are finished, you can say with great pride, **"I made that!"**

BONGO DRUM

Bongo drums are played with your hands. Make this drum and then have fun tapping out a beat.

You'll Need

- ✔ Empty container (coffee can or oatmeal container)
- ✔ Tape (electrical tape or duct tape)
- ✔ Scissors
- ✔ Fabric or paper
- ✔ Glue
- ✔ 3 pieces of canvas
- ✔ Pastels or paints
- ✔ Cord or twine

Wrap tape around the top edge of the container.

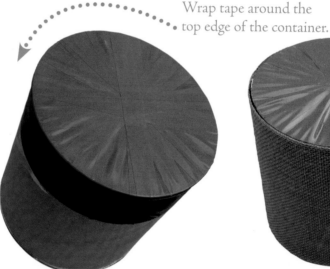

1 Put strips of tape across the top of your container. Pull each strip as tight as you can. Continue until the top of the container is completely covered with tape.

2 Tape around the top edge of the container to help hold the other tape in place.

3 Cut a piece of fabric or paper to cover the container. Put glue on the fabric or paper and then wrap it around the container. Rub the fabric or paper all over so that it sticks well to the container.

4 Draw or paint some decorative shapes on one of your pieces of canvas. Cut the shapes out and glue them to the sides of your container.

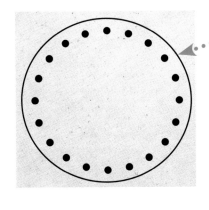

Poke holes through the canvas.

5 Draw a circle on each of the other pieces of canvas. Make them ½ inch (1.3 cm) larger than the top and bottom of your container. Cut out the circles. Poke holes through the canvas close to the outer edges.

Tip When working with scissors, always keep the tip pointed away from your body.

6 Put your two pieces of canvas on the top and bottom of the container. String the cord through a hole on the top canvas and then through a hole on the bottom canvas. Continue to lace your cord through the rest of the holes. Once it is all laced, tighten the cord and then tie the two end pieces together.

9

CASTANETS

Castanets are pairs of shell-shaped clappers that are hinged together with string. They are originally from Spain.

You'll Need

- ✔ Thin cardboard
- ✔ Pencil
- ✔ Scissors
- ✔ Paper for tracing
- ✔ Hole punch
- ✔ Paint, markers or pastels
- ✔ Stickers
- ✔ Buttons, washers, or coins
- ✔ String

Punch holes in the cardboard to match the pattern.

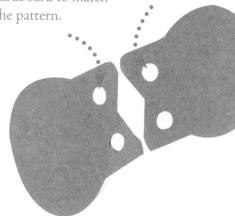

1 Cut a rectangular piece of cardboard sized to 3 x 8 inches (7.5 x 20 cm). Fold the cardboard in half. Trace the template on page 30 onto a piece of paper to create a pattern.

2 Draw around the pattern on the folded cardboard. Cut out the castanet. If it is too difficult to cut through both pieces of the cardboard at the same time, cut one side first, then trace around it and cut the second piece.

3 Separate the two pieces at the top. Punch holes into the top of the castanet as shown by the pattern. Do one side at a time, but make sure the holes line up.

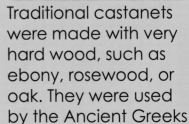

4 Color the pieces of cardboard with paint, markers, or pastels. Decorate the outside with stickers. Glue buttons, washers, or coins on the inside of each side of the cardboard.

Did You Know?

Traditional castanets were made with very hard wood, such as ebony, rosewood, or oak. They were used by the Ancient Greeks and Egyptians.

Make a double knot.

5 Cut a piece of string long enough to loop twice over your thumb. String it through the holes in the cardboard. Tie it once and test it to make sure you can fit your thumb through both loops. Adjust it until it fits and then tie a double knot.

How to play

Let one side of the castanet rest in your palm, with the string looped around your thumb. Strike the other side with your fingertips to knock it against its mate.

TAMBOURINE

The tambourine is a **percussion instrument** that is used in many different kinds of music. It is made of a round frame with bells (called jingles) that ring when you shake it.

You'll Need

- Plastic lid from can
- Paper for tracing
- Cardboard
- Scissors
- Tape
- Metal jingles (10)
- Decorative tape
- 5 finishing nails or toothpicks. If longer than 1¼ inch (3 cm), have an adult trim them to 1¼ inch (3 cm).

Tape pattern together.

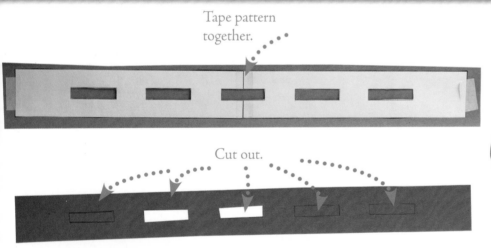

Cut out.

Tape

Tape

Tape

1 Trace the template on page 30 onto a piece of paper twice to create a pattern. Tape this pattern to a piece of thin cardboard.

2 Trace the pattern onto the cardboard. Cut out the large rectangle. Cut out the small rectangles for the jingles.

3 Place the cardboard inside the inner ridge of the plastic lid. Tape it in place.

Wrap tape around the toothpick.

Slide two jingles onto the toothpick.

Did You Know?

The tambourine frame can be left open or covered. To play the tambourine, hit it against your hand or against your leg or hip.

4 Cover the toothpicks or nails with decorative tape. Place each toothpick or nail through two jingles.

Tape

Tape

5 Place the toothpick and jingles on the inside of the cardboard and tape it in place. Repeat until each space has two jingles. Decorate your tambourine. You can paint it or cover it with decorative tape.

Another Idea!

To make your own jingles: gather 10 bottle caps and with an adult's help, flatten them with a hammer. Put the flattened bottle caps on a piece of wood and pound a nail through each one. Pull the nails out. Be careful of the side of the bottle cap that the nail went through. It will have sharp edges.

MARACAS

Maracas are percussion instruments from Latin America. They are made of hollow balls filled with seeds or dried beans that make noise when you shake them.

You'll Need

- ✔ Paper (used paper bag or construction paper)
- ✔ Scissors
- ✔ Masking tape
- ✔ Globe ornament (or round container)
- ✔ Popcorn kernels (or dried rice or beans)
- ✔ Glue
- ✔ Tissue paper

Tape over the hole after adding the popcorn.

Cut a fringe along the top of the paper.

Tape the tube along the edge.

1 Make the handle of the maraca. Cut out a 7 x 12-inch (18 x 31 cm) piece of heavy paper. Make a fringe along the top edge by making 1-inch (2.5 cm) cuts about every ¼ inch (0.6 cm).

2 Roll the paper into a tube shape.

3 Cover the entire globe with tape to make it stronger and easier to decorate. If using an ornament, remove the small top piece. Push a handful of popcorn kernels through the opening of the globe.

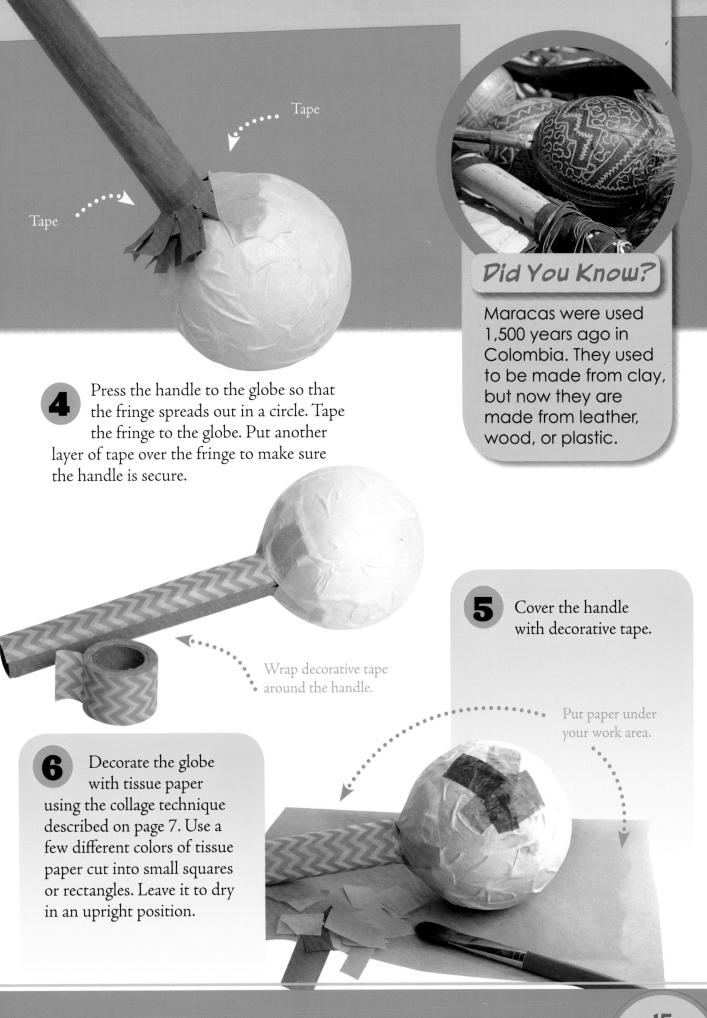

Tape

Tape

Did You Know?

Maracas were used 1,500 years ago in Colombia. They used to be made from clay, but now they are made from leather, wood, or plastic.

4 Press the handle to the globe so that the fringe spreads out in a circle. Tape the fringe to the globe. Put another layer of tape over the fringe to make sure the handle is secure.

5 Cover the handle with decorative tape.

Wrap decorative tape around the handle.

Put paper under your work area.

6 Decorate the globe with tissue paper using the collage technique described on page 7. Use a few different colors of tissue paper cut into small squares or rectangles. Leave it to dry in an upright position.

GUITAR

The guitar is one of the most popular instruments. Most guitars have 6 strings, but some have 4 to 18 strings. Guitars are usually made of different kinds of wood.

You'll Need

- ✔ Pizza box
- ✔ Pencil
- ✔ Paper for tracing
- ✔ Scissors
- ✔ Cardboard
- ✔ Large rubber bands of different widths (6)
- ✔ Cardboard tube (mailing tube or wrapping paper tube)
- ✔ Paint
- ✔ Duct tape
- ✔ Circle stickers

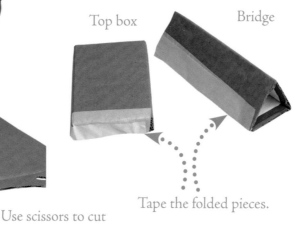

Top box

Bridge

Cut out the front of the tube.

Make two cuts on both sides of the tube.

Tape the folded pieces.

Use scissors to cut out the circle.

1 Unfold the pizza box and lay it flat with the inside facing up. Trace the circle template on page 30 onto a piece of paper to create a pattern. Tape this pattern in the middle of the pizza box. Trace around the pattern.

2 Use the templates on page 31 to cut out two rectangular pieces of cardboard to make a bridge and top box. Fold the bridge piece twice to make a triangular shape and tape it. Fold the top box to make a box shape and tape it.

3 Decorate the pizza box, the top box, the bridge, and the tube with paint or duct tape. Leave them to dry if you painted them. Cut the tube as shown in the illustration.

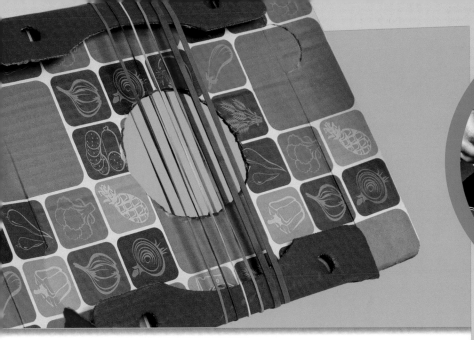

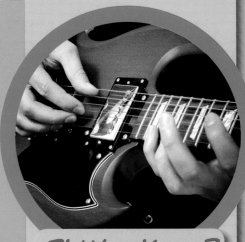

4 Carefully stretch six large rubber bands of different widths over the box and position them over the hole. The different widths will create different sounds. Fold the box back together with the painted side out.

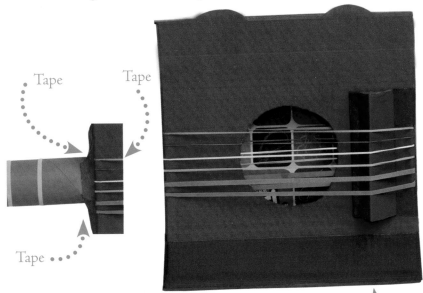

Tape

Tape

Tape

Tape the box closed using duct tape.

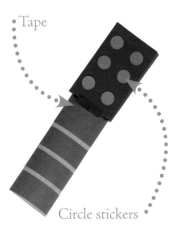

Tape

Circle stickers

5 Tape the side pieces of the tube to the box. Tape the back piece of the tube to the box. Fit the front of the tube under the pizza box and tape it in place. Tape the top box to the tube. Decorate the top box with circle stickers.

6 Pull the rubber bands up and slide the bridge under.

Play a tune!

Strum or pluck the strings with your right hand. At the same time, press against the strings with your left hand. Experiment to make different sounds!

PAN FLUTE

The pan flute or pan pipe is made up of a series of pipes of different lengths. This popular folk instrument is usually made of bamboo.

You'll Need

- ✔ Straws (8)
- ✔ Scissors
- ✔ Air-drying clay
- ✔ Cardboard
- ✔ Craft thread or yarn
- ✔ Tape

Make a mark on the straw with a pencil and then use scissors to cut the straw.

Push a small ball of clay into one end of each straw.

1 Using the pan flute ruler on page 31, mark and cut the straws to each of the marked lengths. The different lengths of straws will create different musical notes.

2 Use a small amount of clay to seal the end of the straw. Tap the end of the straw on a flat surface to make the clay smooth. Make sure there are no holes for air to escape.

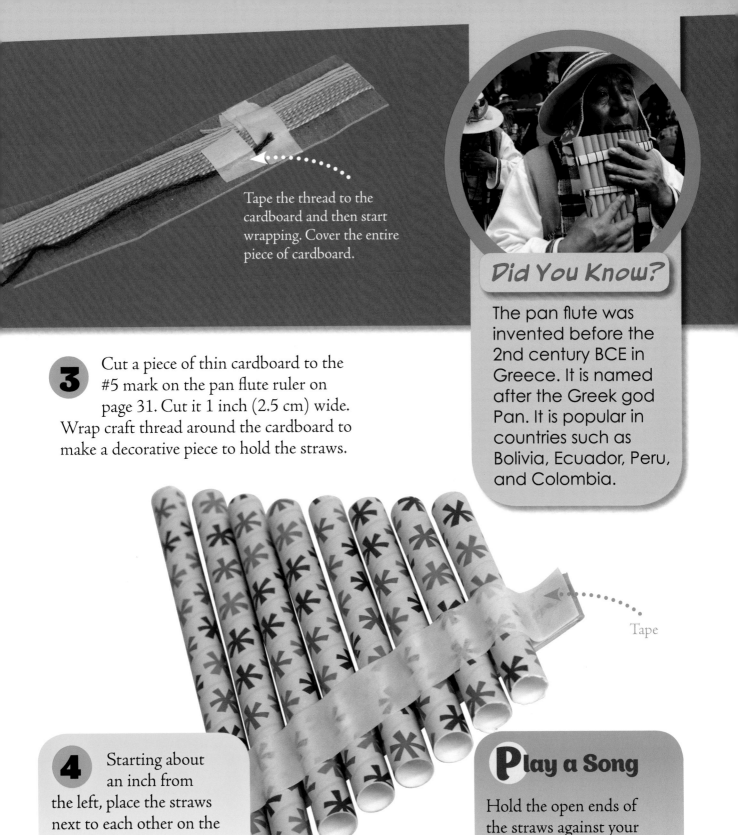

Tape the thread to the cardboard and then start wrapping. Cover the entire piece of cardboard.

3 Cut a piece of thin cardboard to the #5 mark on the pan flute ruler on page 31. Cut it 1 inch (2.5 cm) wide. Wrap craft thread around the cardboard to make a decorative piece to hold the straws.

Tape

4 Starting about an inch from the left, place the straws next to each other on the cardboard in order from longest to shortest. Leave a little room between them to make it easier to play. Tape the straws in place.

Play a Song

Hold the open ends of the straws against your lower lip, and blow across the tops of them. Each straw will make a different note. Try to play a song!

GLOCKENSPIEL

The glockenspiel is made of metal bars arranged like a piano keyboard. It is also called a metallophone.

You'll Need

- ✔ Tin cans (8)
- ✔ Nail
- ✔ Hammer
- ✔ Screwdriver
- ✔ Paper towel tubes
- ✔ Construction paper
- ✔ Scissors
- ✔ Foam core or board for base
- ✔ Duct tape
- ✔ Dowel (small diameter)
- ✔ Rubber bands
- ✔ Washers

Make a hole on each side.

Fold the paper around the can and tape in place.

1 Gather used cans from recycling. Find eight cans that each have a different tone by tapping each can with a spoon or pencil.

2 Have an adult help with this step. **Puncture** the cans near the bottom of the can using a hammer and nail. Make the hole bigger by inserting a screwdriver into the hole and twisting it.

3 Decorate your cans by covering them with construction paper. Lay the can on the construction paper. Make two marks to indicate the length of the can. Cut the paper with scissors.

Tape the stand to the board.

Did You Know?

The xylophone is like a glockenspiel except it is made of wood instead of metal.

4 Make a stand. Place your cans at the one end of your foam core base. Punch holes in two tubes. Cut two pieces of duct tape and cut a fringe around one edge of each piece. Wrap the tape around the end of the tubes without the holes. Tape the tubes to the foam core base on either side of the row of cans.

Turn the can on its side to see the holes when placing them on the dowel.

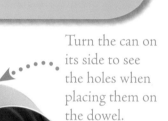

Put a rubber band around the end of each dowel to keep the dowel from slipping out of the holes.

5 Use a dowel long enough to hold all the cans. Place the dowel through the holes on the left tube. Put the can with the deepest sound on the dowel. Place two washers after it. Repeat with all the cans in descending tones.

Play a tune!

Tap the cans with a spoon or pencil to make music!

KAZOO

The kazoo adds a buzzing sound to the player's voice. It is one of the easiest instruments to play. It can be made of plastic, metal, or wood.

You'll Need

- ✔ Cardboard tubes
- ✔ Paint or decorative tape
- ✔ Wax and/or parchment paper
- ✔ Scissors
- ✔ Rubber bands (3)

Make a small hole in the cardboard.

Cut a circle from parchment paper or wax paper.

1 Gather three different sizes of paper tubes from recycling, such as toilet paper rolls, paper towel rolls, or rolls from food wrapping materials.

2 Decorate your tube by painting it or covering it in decorative tape. Make a hole close to one end on one tube. Make the hole in different places on the other tubes to see if it changes the sound.

3 Trace a circle from page 30 onto waxed paper. Using scissors cut it out. Cut one for each tube. If you have parchment paper, cut one of the circles from that.

If the rubber band is big enough, wrap it around twice.

4 Place the waxed paper over one end of each tube. Secure the paper in place using a rubber band. Make sure the paper is held tightly in place.

5 Hum into the open end. Do the different lengths sound different? Does the placement of the hole create a different sound? Do the different papers sound different?

Play a Song

The sound of your voice makes the wax paper vibrate, making it "buzz." Try making different sounds by singing "doo," "who," "rrr," or "brrr" into the kazoo.

SPIN DRUM

The spin drum is a percussion instrument that can be found in many cultures. The handheld drum on a stick has two beads attached to it that hit the center of the drum.

You'll Need

- ✔ Thin cardboard or small round paper-mache box
- ✔ Scissors
- ✔ Hole punch
- ✔ Dowel
- ✔ Masking tape
- ✔ String
- ✔ Large wooden beads (2)
- ✔ Decorative tape or paint

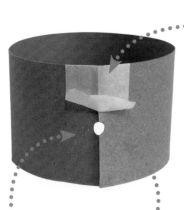

Make a hole.

Tape

Tape

Make a hole.

Knot

Line up the holes.

1 Cut a piece of thin cardboard using the pattern on page 30. Punch a hole with a hole punch in the middle of each end. Line up the holes and tape the ends together.

2 Push the dowel through the hole. Tape it in place. Make a hole on each side of the circle.

3 Cut two 6-inch (15 cm) pieces of string. Tie a knot at one end and thread a bead onto the string. Tie another knot to hold the bead in place.

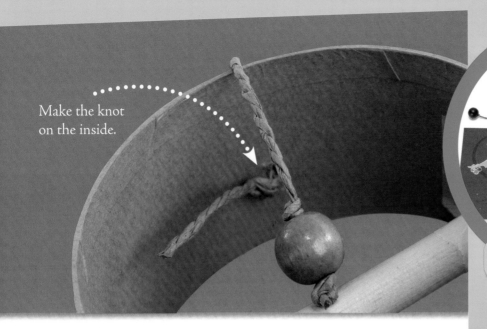

Make the knot on the inside.

Did You Know?

In China they use a spin drum to celebrate the new year.

4 Push the string through the hole on the side of the circle. Make sure the bead reaches the dowel in the center, then tie a double knot on the inside of the circle.

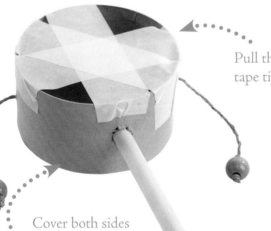

Pull the tape tight.

Cover both sides with tape.

6 Decorate the drum with paint or decorative tape.

5 Tape across both open sides of the circle. Continue until the openings are covered completely with tape.

Tip
If you have a small round paper-mache box you can skip the first step.

Make Some Noise

Spin the handle between the palms of your hand. The beads will bang on the drum like drumsticks. Spin your drum!

RAIN STICK

A rain stick is a long, hollow tube partially filled with small pebbles or beans that has small pins or thorns arranged on its inside surface.

You'll Need

- ✔ Cardboard tube
- ✔ Pushpin or small nail
- ✔ Toothpicks (pointed at one end only)
- ✔ Parchment or wax paper
- ✔ Rubber bands (2)
- ✔ Masking tape
- ✔ Grains (uncooked rice and/or lentils)
- ✔ Paint, decorative tape, construction paper, or tissue paper
- ✔ String or yarn

The more toothpicks the better your rain stick will sound!

The tube should be the same diameter as a toothpick.

Cover the outside of the tube with masking tape.

1 Make holes at the top of the cardboard tube by pushing a pushpin or nail through the cardboard. Wiggle it a bit to make the hole bigger before removing it from the cardboard.

2 Push a toothpick through the hole started with the pin. Push it all the way to the other side. Repeat this step, alternating sides until you get to the bottom.

3 Use the pattern on page 30 to trace two circles on parchment or wax paper. Cut them out. Place one paper circle over one end of the tube. Secure with a rubber band. Cover the edges with masking tape. Then cover the entire tube with masking tape.

4 Fill the tube with a small bowl full of an assortment of grains.

Did You Know?

South American rain sticks are made from dried cactus.

5 Place the other paper circle over the other end and secure it with a rubber band and tape.

6 Decorate your rain stick. Paint it, cover it with decorative tape, construction paper, or tissue paper using the collage technique described on page 7. Wrap some string, yarn, or a bracelet around the top.

Listen to this!

Tip the rain stick so the grains fall to the other end of the tube. It sounds like rain!

JINGLE STICKS

Jingle sticks are a Latin percussion instrument. They are like a tambourine on a stick.

You'll Need

- Cardboard
- Paper for tracing
- Scissors
- Decorative tape (or paint)
- Stickers (optional)
- Pushpin or nail
- Pipe cleaners (3)
- Bells (9)
- Duct tape
- Dowel stick

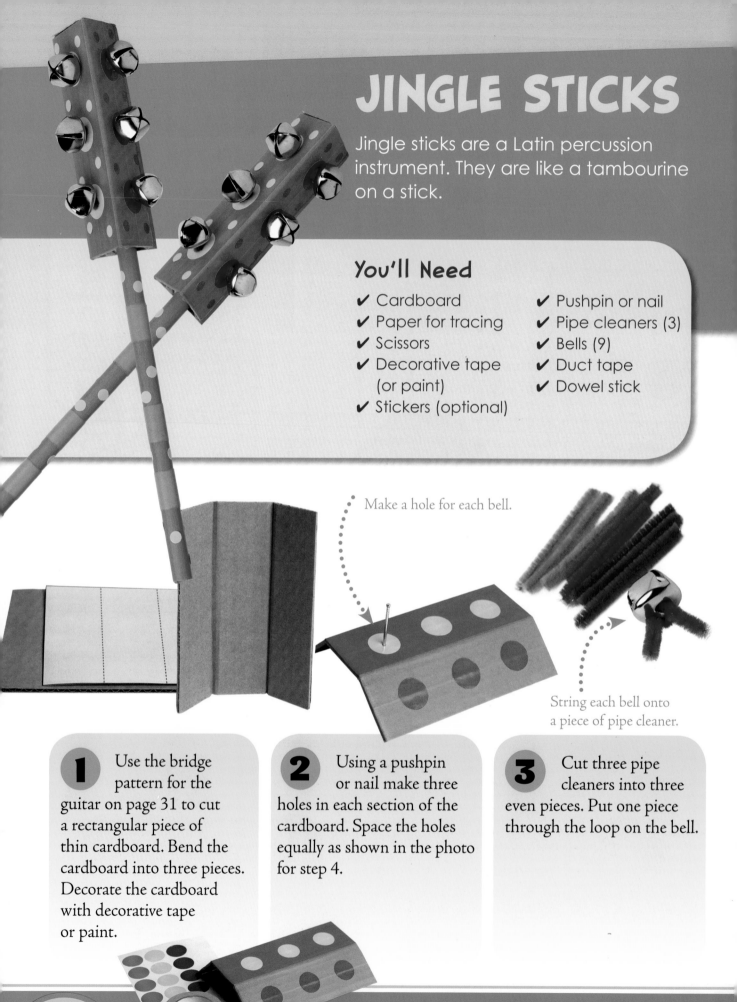

Make a hole for each bell.

String each bell onto a piece of pipe cleaner.

1 Use the bridge pattern for the guitar on page 31 to cut a rectangular piece of thin cardboard. Bend the cardboard into three pieces. Decorate the cardboard with decorative tape or paint.

2 Using a pushpin or nail make three holes in each section of the cardboard. Space the holes equally as shown in the photo for step 4.

3 Cut three pipe cleaners into three even pieces. Put one piece through the loop on the bell.

Did You Know?

A jingle bell or sleigh bell makes a distinctive jingle sound, especially in large numbers.

Tape the edges together.

4 Attach the bells to the cardboard by pushing the ends of the pipe cleaners through the hole. Tape in place. Repeat with all the bells.

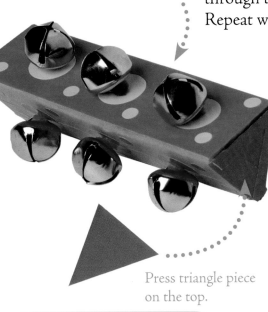

Press triangle piece on the top.

Tape across the opening after adding the paper.

5 Fold the cardboard and tape the two ends together. Cut a triangle out of tape to fit the top. Place the triangle over the top.

Tip
Stickers are a great option for decorating the jingle sticks.

6 Decorate a dowel stick with decorative tape. Insert it into the cardboard box. Add some paper to make it fit snuggly. Tape across the bottom to hold it in place.

PATTERNS

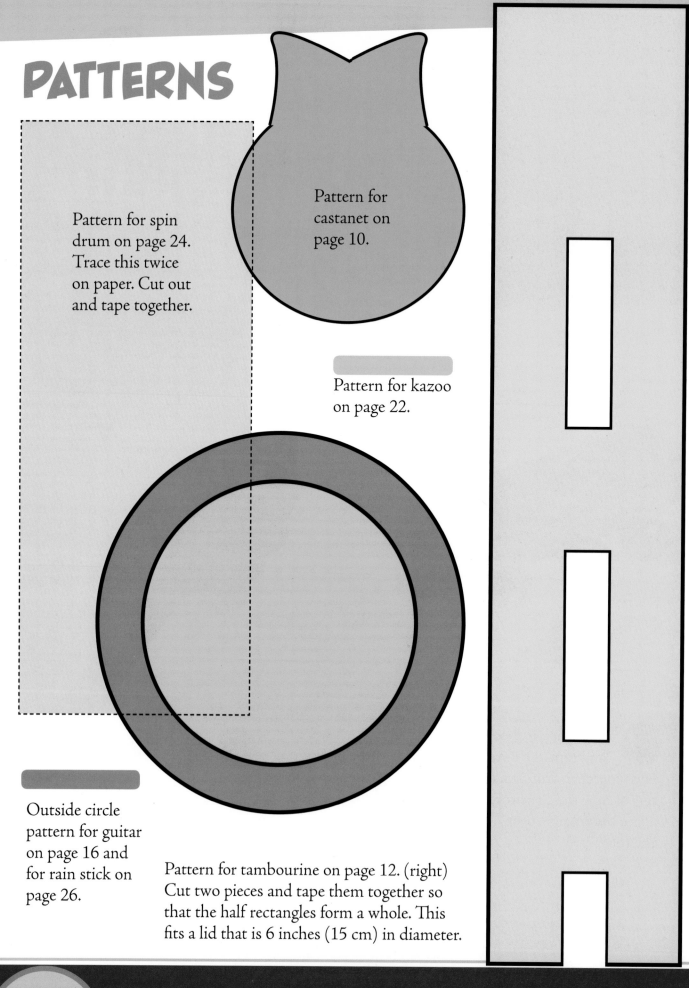

Pattern for spin drum on page 24. Trace this twice on paper. Cut out and tape together.

Pattern for castanet on page 10.

Pattern for kazoo on page 22.

Outside circle pattern for guitar on page 16 and for rain stick on page 26.

Pattern for tambourine on page 12. (right) Cut two pieces and tape them together so that the half rectangles form a whole. This fits a lid that is 6 inches (15 cm) in diameter.

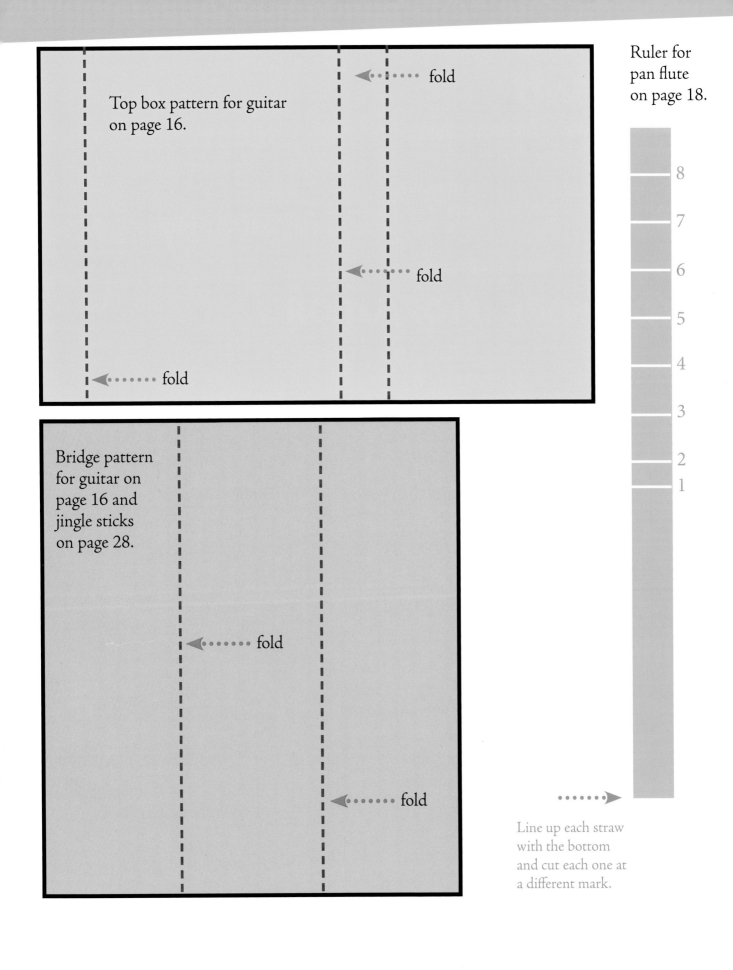

Top box pattern for guitar
on page 16.

fold

fold

fold

Ruler for
pan flute
on page 18.

8
7
6
5
4
3
2
1

Bridge pattern
for guitar on
page 16 and
jingle sticks
on page 28.

fold

fold

Line up each straw
with the bottom
and cut each one at
a different mark.

GLOSSARY

dowel A wooden peg used to hold pieces together.

percussion instrument A musical instrument sounded by striking, shaking, or scraping.

puncture To create a hole in something.

retract To draw back in.

score To cut or scratch a line into a surface.

template A shape used as a pattern.

FOR MORE INFORMATION

FURTHER READING

DK Publishing. *The Big Book of Crafts and Activities.* New York, NY: DK Publishing, 2013.

DK Publishing. *Children's Book of Music.* New York, NY: DK Publishing, 2010.

Kingloff, Amanda. *Project Kid: 100 Ingenious Crafts for Family Fun.* New York, NY: Artisan, 2014.

WEBSITES

For web resources related to the subject of this book, go to: www.windmillbooks.com/weblinks and select this book's title.

INDEX